Out on the wide sea it was noisy and busy.

Instead of stacks and skerries and the comfort of cosy nest burrows, the expansive water stretched out without a glimpse of land in sight.

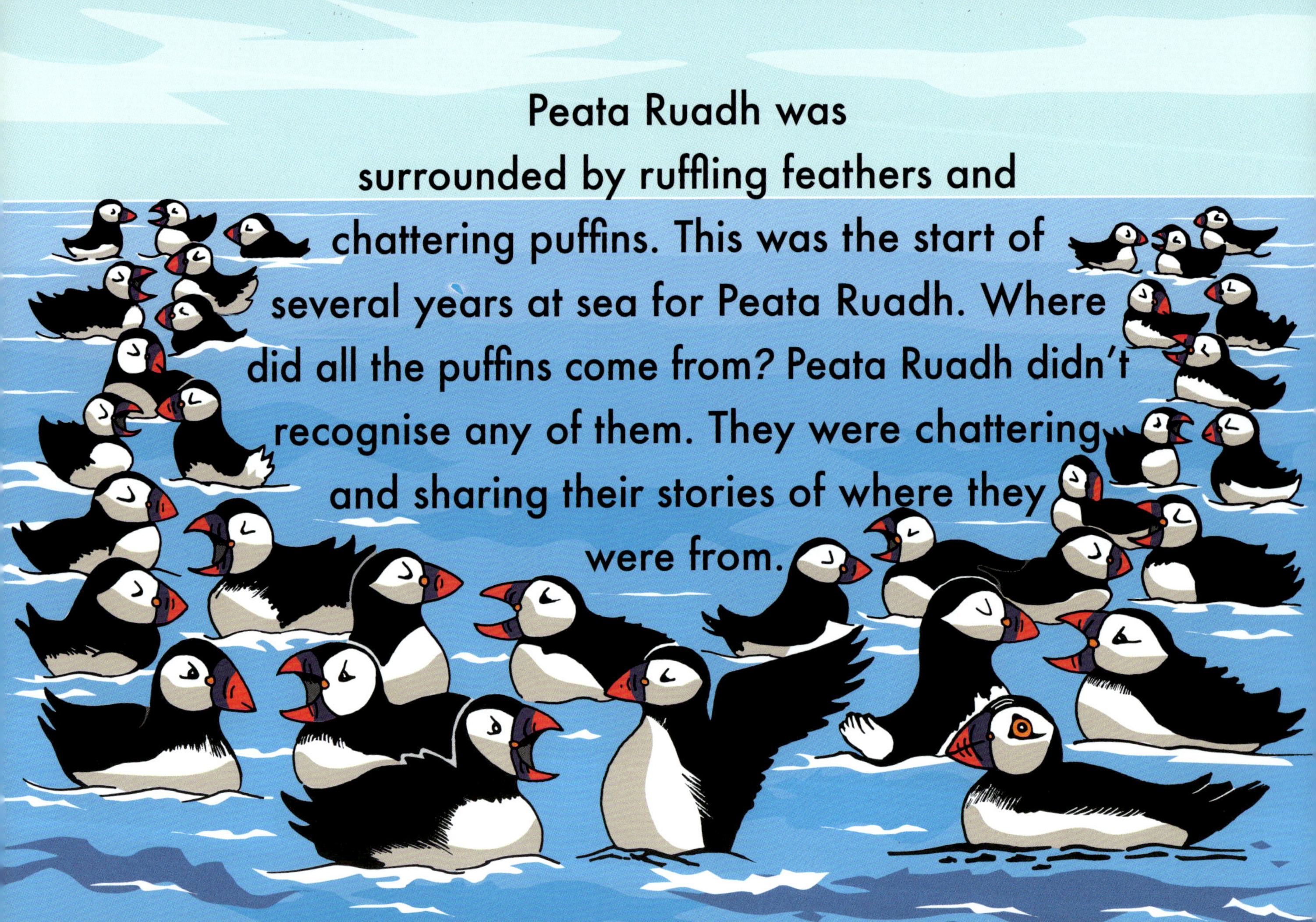

Peata Ruadh was
surrounded by ruffling feathers and
chattering puffins. This was the start of
several years at sea for Peata Ruadh. Where
did all the puffins come from? Peata Ruadh didn't
recognise any of them. They were chattering
and sharing their stories of where they
were from.

Peata Ruadh went fishing in the daylight
for his favourite silvery sandeels.
They made him feel healthy and
full. But when there were not
so many sandeels to be
found he had to
make do with the
other little fish.

Every day, the puffins would help each other to remember how to keep safe when they fished. They chanted in the hope they would remember what to look out for in the water. They didn't want to catch a bellyfull of plastic. They knew what could happen to them if they were not careful.

Plastic rings
Plastic bags
Brightly coloured plastic toys

Plastic straws
Plastic plates
Man-made plastic fibre clothes

Plastic packaging
Plastic bottles
Shiny plastic coated paper

At the end of a busy day when the puffins were bobbing on top of the water a puffin called Tammie Norrie began to tell his story.

"I long for my cosy warm burrow away from this bitterly cold wind." began Tammie Norrie.

"I share the cliff tops with Shetland sheep. They have lived on the cliff tops since the time of the vikings."

"What do they look like?" piped up a little Norwegian puffin called Lundefugl, as she came closer to listen.

"They have white or brown fluffy bodies. They have four very thin legs and pointy ears." replied Tammie Norrie.

"They leave clumps of their beautiful wool across the cliffs and I spend lovely afternoons finding and gathering the soft wool."

"Why do you do that?" asked Peata Ruadh.

"I use it in my burrow to help keep me warm." explained Tammie Norrie. "It is good to spend your time gathering things that are useful."

"I do remember I had something soft in my burrow and it was very warm." whispered Peata Ruadh, now understanding.

It had been a successful few days fishing, although there had been a great amount of dodging floating debris and avoiding sinking bits of castaway plastics. The puffins continued to chant their song together. *"My relatives have told stories for generations about an island once known as the Longship island."* began a puffin called Poc'han.

"Boats still come to the island bringing visitors." he continued.

Lundefugl was close by and spoke up asking "How do you know this?"

"My relatives tell me that every day longships still arrive on the shores and people walk up the cliffsides to the flat grassy tops." said Poc'han. "The people sit very still. They get really close to us and watch what we do. I think they like that."

"Why are you telling us this story?" asked Peata Ruadh.

"Because we should encourage these visitors to see how special we are and how much help we need if we are to fish safely in the seas again. And show them how much help we need if we are to continue to return to build nests and bring up our own pufflings." explained Poc'han.

"Do they understand how special we are?" asked Lundefugl.

"I hope they do, they sit watching us for as long as there is daylight. Then they come back again the next day." Poc'han explained.

"Well...," sighed Lundefugl, *"it is important that we encourage visitors. We must explain how dangerous the sea is."*
"And how we long for the seas to be clean and safe again." added Peata Ruadh.

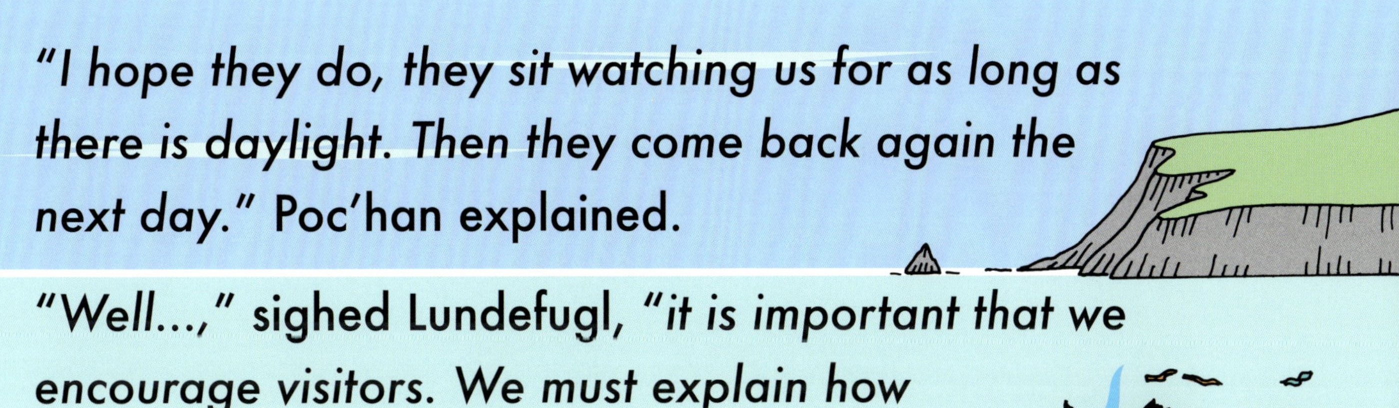

It was a bitterly cold night with the waves rising and falling with the howling wind. The raft of puffins gathered for another long night.

"*I can't stop shivering!*" complained Peata Ruadh to Lundefugl, his feathers shaking in the cold.

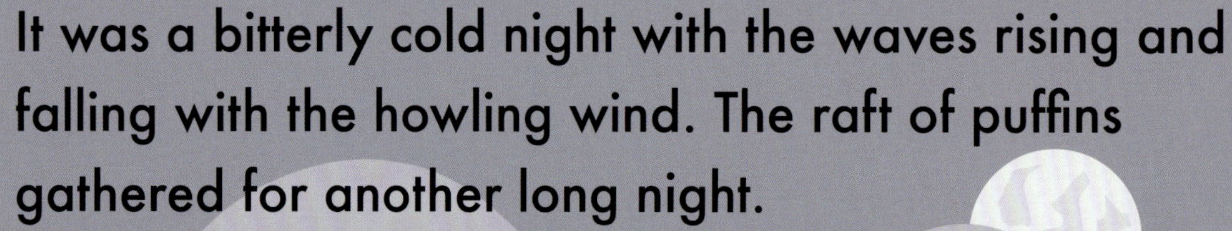

"This is just like home!" said Lundi, the Icelandic puffin.
"My feet are always warmer than my head."

"What is home like?" asked Peata Ruadh.

Lundi described how his home was engulfed in billowing hot steamy clouds from geysers.

"My burrow is close to the steamy clouds and it is warm and cosy. Every burrow is! The ground heats our burrows!" said Lundi dreamily.

Peata Ruadh whispered *"That is ingenious to use the heat from the ground to keep warm."*

"Sometimes we get so warm we have to cool off on the glaciers!" Lundi laughed.

The snowstorm was raging, huge flakes fell from the sky landing in feathery patterns on the water. Soon all the puffins were covered in a feathery layer of snowflakes.

"I have lost most of my wing feathers in my moult and I am freezing cold!" shivered Lundefugl.

"*If we all huddle together the snow will make a blanket over us!*" laughed Peata Ruadh.

The puffins huddled under the snow blanket to save energy and get as warm as they could.

"My mother told me how she would pluck the softest feathers from her chest to make a little bed for her puffling, then how her soft feathers would help to make blankets." began Lundefugl.

"A puffin blanket?" said Peata Ruadh with interest.

"It is really called a duvet." explained Lundefugl.

"My mother shared the Island of Lånan with eider ducks. They have little wooden houses made especially for them. In return, after their chicks have left, the downy feathers are gathered by people."

"Why?" asked Peata Ruadh.

"They are the finest, softest feathers and very warm. They are collected and made into an eiderdown blanket called a duvet." explained Lundefugl.

"Many eiderdown feathers are needed to make a duvet. One year there were not enough eiderdown feathers. My mother gave her nesting down feathers in return for the safety of her puffling." Lundefugl proudly said.

"So eiderdown was mixed with puffin down to make the duvets." Lundefugl explained.

"That was a really clever idea to keep warm and help each other!" commented Peata Ruadh.

Peata Ruadh's first years out at sea were nearly over.
The days were getting longer and the
temperatures were getting warmer.
Peata Ruadh, Lundefugl, Lundi, Poc'han, Tammie
Norrie and all the other puffins in the raft bobbed
about on top of the water and began to feel that it
would soon be time to leave the big wide sea.

Together, they chanted,
hoping that something would
change before it was too late.